Are you enjoy awesome Wine

C000133228

If so, please leave us a review. We are very interested in your feedback to create even better products for you to enjoy in the near future.

**Shopping for Weekly & Monthly Planners can be fun.
Visit our website at amazing-notebooks.com or scan the QR code below to see all of our awesome and creative products!**

Thank you very much!

Amazing Notebooks & Journals

www.amazing-notebooks.com

Welcome to Your Wine Journal

Name . . . .

Phone . . . .

Email . . . .

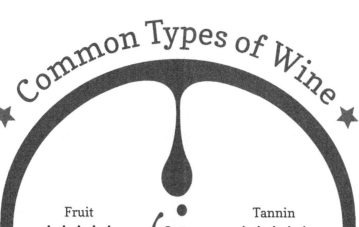

Fruit		Tannin
★ ★ ★ ★ ☆		★ ★ ★ ★ ☆
Body		Acidity
★ ★ ★ ★ ★		★ ★ ☆ ☆ ☆

Cabernet Sauvignon

"Kab-er-nay Saw-vin-yawn"

Taste: Black Cherry, Black Currant, Baking Spices, and Cedar (from oak)

Style: Full-Bodied Red Wine

Description: Cabernet Sauvignon is a full-bodied red grape first heavily planted in the Bordeaux region. Today, it's the most popular wine variety in the world! Wines are full-bodied with bold tannins and a long persistent finish driven mostly by the higher levels of alcohol and tannin that often accompany these wines.

Food Pairing: lamb, beef, smoked meats, French, American, firm cheeses like aged cheddar and hard cheeses like Pecorino.

Fruit
★★★★☆

Body
★★★★★

Tannin
★★⯨☆☆

Acidity
★★★★☆

Syrah
"Sear-ah"

Taste: Blueberry, plum, tobacco, cured meat, black pepper, violet

Style: Full-Bodied Red Wine

Description: Syrah (aka Shiraz) is a full-bodied red wine that's heavily planted in the Rhône Valley in France and Australia. The wines have intense fruit flavors and medium-weight tannins. Syrah is commonly blended with Grenache and Mourvèdre to create the red Rhône blend. The wine often has a meaty (beef broth, jerky) quality.

Food Pairing: lamb, beef, smoked meats; Mediterranean, French, and American firm cheeses like white cheddar, and hard cheeses like Spanish Manchego.

Fruit		Tannin
★★★★★		★★⯪☆☆
Body		Acidity
★★★★★		★★☆☆☆

Zinfandel

"Zin-fan-dell"

Taste: A broad, exotic array of fruits from stone (overripe nectarine), to red (raspberry, sour cherry), to blue (plum, blueberry), to black (blackberry, boysenberry), Asian 5 Spice Powder, Sweet Tobacco

Style: Medium-bodied to full-bodied Red Wine

Description: Zinfandel is a medium-bodied red wine that originated in Croatia. Wines are fruit-forward and spicy with a medium length finish. Zinfandel is a red grape that may be better known in its pink variation, White Zinfandel.

Food Pairing: chicken, pork, cured meat, lamb, beef, barbecue, Italian, American, Chinese, Thai, Indian, full-flavored like cheddar and firm cheeses such as Manchego.

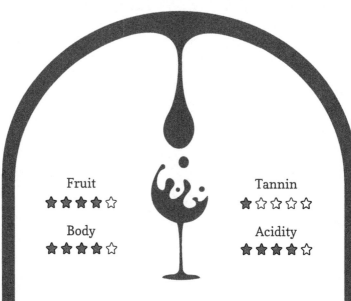

Fruit
★★★★☆

Body
★★★★☆

Tannin
★☆☆☆☆

Acidity
★★★★☆

Pinot Noir

"Pee-no Nwar"

Taste: Very red fruited (cherry, cranberry) and red-floral (rose), often with appealing vegetal notes of beet, rhubarb, or mushroom

Style: Lighter-bodied Red Wine

Description: Pinot Noir is a dry, light-bodied red that was first widely planted in France. The wines typically have higher acidity and soft a soft, smooth, low-tannin finish.

Food Pairing: chicken, pork, veal, duck, cured meat, French, German, cream sauces, soft cheeses, nutty medium-firm cheeses like Gruyère.

Fruit
★ ★ ★ ★ ☆

Sweetness
✩ ✩ ✩ ✩ ✩

Body
★ ★ ★ ★ ☆

Acidity
★ ★ ⯪ ☆ ☆

Chardonnay

"Shar-dun-nay"

Taste: Yellow citrus (Meyer lemon), yellow pomaceous fruits (like yellow pear and apple), tropical fruits (banana, pineapple), and often a touch of butterscotch, vanilla or toasted caramel notes from oak

Style: Medium- to Full-Bodied White Wine.

Description: Chardonnay is a dry full-bodied white wine that was planted in large quantities for the first time in France. When oak-aged, Chardonnay will have spicy, bourbon-y notes. Unoaked wines are lighter and zesty with apple and citrus flavors. Chardonnay is the white grape of Burgundy.

Food Pairing: lobster, crab, shrimp, chicken, pork, mushroom, French, cream sauces, soft cheeses such as triple cream brie, medium-firm cheeses like Gruyère

Fruit
★ ★ ★ ★ ★

Body
★ ★ ☆ ☆ ☆

Sweetness
★ ☆ ☆ ☆ ☆

Acidity
★ ★ ★ ★ ★

Sauvignon Blanc

"Saw-vin-yawn Blonk"

Taste: Aggressively-citrus-driven (grapefruit pith), with some exotic fruits (honeydew melon, passion fruit, kiwi) and always an herbaceous quality (grass, mint, green pepper).

Style: Light- to Medium-Bodied White Wine.

Description: Sauvignon Blanc is a dry white grape first widely planted in France. Wines are tart, typically with herbal, "green" fruit flavors.

Food Pairing: fish, chicken, pork, veal, Mexican, Vietnamese, French, herb-crusted goat cheese, nutty cheeses such as Gruyère.

Fruit
★★☆☆☆

Sweetness
★☆☆☆☆

Body
★☆☆☆☆

Acidity
★★★☆☆

Pinot Gris

"Pee-no Gree"

Taste: Delicate citrus (lime water, orange zest) and pomaceous fruits (apple skin, pear sauce), white floral notes, and cheese rind (from lees usage).

Style: Light-Bodied White Wine.

Description: Pinot Gris is a dry light-bodied white grape that is planted heavily in Italy, but also in France and Germany. Wines are light to middle-weight and easy drinking, often with some bitter flavor on the palate (bitter almond, quinine).

Food Pairing: Salad, delicate poached fish, light and mild cheeses.

Fruit
★ ★ ★ ★ ★

Body
★ ★ ☆ ☆ ☆

Sweetness
★ ★ ★ ☆ ☆

Acidity
★ ★ ★ ★ ★

Riesling
"Reese-ling"

Taste: Citrus (kefir lime, lemon juice) and stone-fruit (white peach, nectarine) always feature prominently, although there are also usually floral and sweet herbal elements as well.

Style: Floral and fruit-driven aromatic white that comes in variable sweetness. Some producers choose not to ferment all the grape sugar and therefore make the wine in an "off-dry" style.

Description: Always very high in acid, when made as a table wine Rieslings can be harmoniously sweet (sweet and sour) or dry (very acidic). The wine is polarizing because some people find dry styles too acidic and sweet styles too cloying, but sweetness is always a wine making decision and not inherent to the grape.

Food Pairing: chicken, pork, duck, turkey, cured meat, Indian, Thai, Vietnamese, Moroccan, German, washed-rind cheeses and fondue.

Wine Name _____

Winery _____ Region _____

When _____ Price _____ Alcohol % _____

Appearance _____ ♟ ♟ ♟ ♟ ♟

Aroma _____ ♟ ♟ ♟ ♟ ♟

Body _____ ♟ ♟ ♟ ♟ ♟

Taste _____ ♟ ♟ ♟ ♟ ♟

Finish _____ ♟ ♟ ♟ ♟ ♟

—— Pairs With ——   Serving Temperature   —— Taste ——

—— Review / Notes ——

_____
_____
_____
_____
_____
_____
_____
_____
_____

Ratings ☆ ☆ ☆ ☆ ☆

Wine Name _____

Winery _____ Region _____

When _____ Price _____ Alcohol % _____

Appearance _____ ♀♀♀♀♀

Aroma _____ ♀♀♀♀♀

Body _____ ♀♀♀♀♀

Taste _____ ♀♀♀♀♀

Finish _____ ♀♀♀♀♀

Pairs With

Serving Temperature

Taste

Review / Notes

_____
_____
_____
_____
_____
_____
_____
_____
_____
_____

Ratings ☆ ☆ ☆ ☆ ☆

Wine Name _____

Winery _____ Region _____

When _____ Price _____ Alcohol % _____

Appearance _____ ♟ ♟ ♟ ♟ ♟

Aroma _____ ♟ ♟ ♟ ♟ ♟

Body _____ ♟ ♟ ♟ ♟ ♟

Taste _____ ♟ ♟ ♟ ♟ ♟

Finish _____ ♟ ♟ ♟ ♟ ♟

──── Pairs With ────   ── Serving Temperature ──   ──── Taste ────

──────────────────── Review / Notes ────────────────────

_____

_____

_____

_____

_____

_____

_____

_____

_____

Ratings ☆ ☆ ☆ ☆ ☆

Wine Name _____

Winery _____ Region _____

When _____ Price _____ Alcohol % _____

Appearance _____ ♟ ♟ ♟ ♟ ♟

Aroma _____ ♟ ♟ ♟ ♟ ♟

Body _____ ♟ ♟ ♟ ♟ ♟

Taste _____ ♟ ♟ ♟ ♟ ♟

Finish _____ ♟ ♟ ♟ ♟ ♟

Pairs With

Serving Temperature

Taste

Review / Notes

_____
_____
_____
_____
_____
_____
_____
_____
_____
_____

Ratings ☆ ☆ ☆ ☆ ☆

Wine Name _____

Winery _____ Region _____

When _____ Price _____ Alcohol % _____

Appearance _____ 🍷 🍷 🍷 🍷 🍷

Aroma _____ 🍷 🍷 🍷 🍷 🍷

Body _____ 🍷 🍷 🍷 🍷 🍷

Taste _____ 🍷 🍷 🍷 🍷 🍷

Finish _____ 🍷 🍷 🍷 🍷 🍷

Pairs With

Serving Temperature

Taste

Review / Notes

_____
_____
_____
_____
_____
_____
_____
_____
_____
_____

Ratings ☆ ☆ ☆ ☆ ☆

Wine Name _____

Winery _____ Region _____

When _____ Price _____ Alcohol % _____

Appearance _____ ♥♥♥♥♥
Aroma _____ ♥♥♥♥♥
Body _____ ♥♥♥♥♥
Taste _____ ♥♥♥♥♥
Finish _____ ♥♥♥♥♥

Pairs With

Serving Temperature

Taste

Review / Notes

_____
_____
_____
_____
_____
_____
_____
_____
_____
_____

Ratings ☆ ☆ ☆ ☆ ☆

Wine Name _____

Winery _____ Region _____

When _____ Price _____ Alcohol % _____

Appearance _____ 🍷 🍷 🍷 🍷 🍷

Aroma _____ 🍷 🍷 🍷 🍷 🍷

Body _____ 🍷 🍷 🍷 🍷 🍷

Taste _____ 🍷 🍷 🍷 🍷 🍷

Finish _____ 🍷 🍷 🍷 🍷 🍷

Pairs With

Serving Temperature

Taste

Review / Notes

_____
_____
_____
_____
_____
_____
_____
_____
_____

Ratings ☆ ☆ ☆ ☆ ☆

Wine Name _____

Winery _____ Region _____

When _____ Price _____ Alcohol % _____

Appearance _____ ♎ ♎ ♎ ♎ ♎

Aroma _____ ♎ ♎ ♎ ♎ ♎

Body _____ ♎ ♎ ♎ ♎ ♎

Taste _____ ♎ ♎ ♎ ♎ ♎

Finish _____ ♎ ♎ ♎ ♎ ♎

--- Pairs With ---

--- Serving Temperature ---

--- Taste ---

--- Review / Notes ---

_____
_____
_____
_____
_____
_____
_____
_____
_____
_____

Ratings ☆ ☆ ☆ ☆ ☆

Wine Name _____

Winery _____ Region _____

When _____ Price _____ Alcohol % _____

Appearance _____ 🍷 🍷 🍷 🍷 🍷

Aroma _____ 🍷 🍷 🍷 🍷 🍷

Body _____ 🍷 🍷 🍷 🍷 🍷

Taste _____ 🍷 🍷 🍷 🍷 🍷

Finish _____ 🍷 🍷 🍷 🍷 🍷

―――― Pairs With ――――   Serving
                        Temperature   ―――― Taste ――――

―――――――― Review / Notes ――――――――

_____
_____
_____
_____
_____
_____
_____
_____
_____
_____

Ratings ☆ ☆ ☆ ☆ ☆

Wine Name _____

Winery _____ Region _____

When _____ Price _____ Alcohol % _____

Appearance _____ ♙ ♙ ♙ ♙ ♙

Aroma _____ ♙ ♙ ♙ ♙ ♙

Body _____ ♙ ♙ ♙ ♙ ♙

Taste _____ ♙ ♙ ♙ ♙ ♙

Finish _____ ♙ ♙ ♙ ♙ ♙

── Pairs With ──   ── Serving Temperature ──   ── Taste ──

── Review / Notes ──

_____
_____
_____
_____
_____
_____
_____
_____
_____
_____

Ratings ☆ ☆ ☆ ☆ ☆

Wine Name _____

Winery _____ Region _____

When _____ Price _____ Alcohol % _____

Appearance _____ 🍷 🍷 🍷 🍷 🍷

Aroma _____ 🍷 🍷 🍷 🍷 🍷

Body _____ 🍷 🍷 🍷 🍷 🍷

Taste _____ 🍷 🍷 🍷 🍷 🍷

Finish _____ 🍷 🍷 🍷 🍷 🍷

—— Pairs With ——

—— Serving Temperature ——

—— Taste ——

———— Review / Notes ————

_____
_____
_____
_____
_____
_____
_____
_____
_____
_____

Ratings ☆ ☆ ☆ ☆ ☆

Wine Name _____

Winery _____ Region _____

When _____ Price _____ Alcohol % _____

Appearance _____ ♟ ♟ ♟ ♟ ♟

Aroma _____ ♟ ♟ ♟ ♟ ♟

Body _____ ♟ ♟ ♟ ♟ ♟

Taste _____ ♟ ♟ ♟ ♟ ♟

Finish _____ ♟ ♟ ♟ ♟ ♟

Pairs With

Serving Temperature

Taste

Review / Notes

_____
_____
_____
_____
_____
_____
_____
_____
_____
_____

Ratings ☆ ☆ ☆ ☆ ☆

Wine Name _____

Winery _____ Region _____

When _____ Price _____ Alcohol % _____

Appearance _____ ♟ ♟ ♟ ♟ ♟

Aroma _____ ♟ ♟ ♟ ♟ ♟

Body _____ ♟ ♟ ♟ ♟ ♟

Taste _____ ♟ ♟ ♟ ♟ ♟

Finish _____ ♟ ♟ ♟ ♟ ♟

Pairs With	Serving Temperature	Taste

Review / Notes

_____
_____
_____
_____
_____
_____
_____
_____
_____

Ratings ☆ ☆ ☆ ☆ ☆

Wine Name _____

Winery _____ Region _____

When _____ Price _____ Alcohol % _____

Appearance _____ 🍷 🍷 🍷 🍷 🍷

Aroma _____ 🍷 🍷 🍷 🍷 🍷

Body _____ 🍷 🍷 🍷 🍷 🍷

Taste _____ 🍷 🍷 🍷 🍷 🍷

Finish _____ 🍷 🍷 🍷 🍷 🍷

Pairs With

Serving Temperature

Taste

Review / Notes

_____
_____
_____
_____
_____
_____
_____
_____
_____
_____
_____

Ratings ☆ ☆ ☆ ☆ ☆

Wine Name _____

Winery _____ Region _____

When _____ Price _____ Alcohol % _____

Appearance _____ ♟ ♟ ♟ ♟ ♟

Aroma _____ ♟ ♟ ♟ ♟ ♟

Body _____ ♟ ♟ ♟ ♟ ♟

Taste _____ ♟ ♟ ♟ ♟ ♟

Finish _____ ♟ ♟ ♟ ♟ ♟

―――― Pairs With ―――― ―― Serving Temperature ―― ―――― Taste ――――

――――――――――――――――――― Review / Notes ―――――――――――――――――――

_____

_____

_____

_____

_____

_____

_____

_____

_____

Ratings ☆ ☆ ☆ ☆ ☆

Wine Name _____

Winery _____ Region _____

When _____ Price _____ Alcohol % _____

Appearance _____ ♀ ♀ ♀ ♀ ♀

Aroma _____ ♀ ♀ ♀ ♀ ♀

Body _____ ♀ ♀ ♀ ♀ ♀

Taste _____ ♀ ♀ ♀ ♀ ♀

Finish _____ ♀ ♀ ♀ ♀ ♀

Pairs With	Serving Temperature	Taste

Review / Notes

_____

_____

_____

_____

_____

_____

_____

_____

_____

_____

Ratings ☆ ☆ ☆ ☆ ☆

Wine Name _____

Winery _____ Region _____

When _____ Price _____ Alcohol % _____

Appearance _____ ♀♀♀♀♀

Aroma _____ ♀♀♀♀♀

Body _____ ♀♀♀♀♀

Taste _____ ♀♀♀♀♀

Finish _____ ♀♀♀♀♀

Pairs With

Serving Temperature

Taste

Review / Notes

_____
_____
_____
_____
_____
_____
_____
_____
_____
_____

Ratings ☆ ☆ ☆ ☆ ☆

Wine Name _____

Winery _____ Region _____

When _____ Price _____ Alcohol % _____

Appearance _____ 🍷 🍷 🍷 🍷 🍷

Aroma _____ 🍷 🍷 🍷 🍷 🍷

Body _____ 🍷 🍷 🍷 🍷 🍷

Taste _____ 🍷 🍷 🍷 🍷 🍷

Finish _____ 🍷 🍷 🍷 🍷 🍷

Pairs With

Serving Temperature

Taste

Review / Notes

_____
_____
_____
_____
_____
_____
_____
_____
_____
_____

Ratings ☆ ☆ ☆ ☆ ☆

Wine Name _____

Winery _____ Region _____

When _____ Price _____ Alcohol % _____

Appearance _____ ♟ ♟ ♟ ♟ ♟
Aroma _____ ♟ ♟ ♟ ♟ ♟
Body _____ ♟ ♟ ♟ ♟ ♟
Taste _____ ♟ ♟ ♟ ♟ ♟
Finish _____ ♟ ♟ ♟ ♟ ♟

——— Pairs With ———

——— Serving Temperature ———

——— Taste ———

——————— Review / Notes ———————

_____
_____
_____
_____
_____
_____
_____
_____
_____

Ratings ☆ ☆ ☆ ☆ ☆

Wine Name _____

Winery _____ Region _____

When _____ Price _____ Alcohol % _____

Appearance _____ ♟ ♟ ♟ ♟ ♟

Aroma _____ ♟ ♟ ♟ ♟ ♟

Body _____ ♟ ♟ ♟ ♟ ♟

Taste _____ ♟ ♟ ♟ ♟ ♟

Finish _____ ♟ ♟ ♟ ♟ ♟

--- Pairs With ---

--- Serving Temperature ---

--- Taste ---

--- Review / Notes ---

_____

_____

_____

_____

_____

_____

_____

_____

_____

_____

Ratings ☆ ☆ ☆ ☆ ☆

Wine Name _____

Winery _____ Region _____

When _____ Price _____ Alcohol % _____

Appearance _____ ♥ ♥ ♥ ♥ ♥
Aroma _____ ♥ ♥ ♥ ♥ ♥
Body _____ ♥ ♥ ♥ ♥ ♥
Taste _____ ♥ ♥ ♥ ♥ ♥
Finish _____ ♥ ♥ ♥ ♥ ♥

—— Pairs With —— ┌ Serving Temperature ┐ —— Taste ——

—————————————— Review / Notes ——————————————

_____
_____
_____
_____
_____
_____
_____
_____
_____

Ratings ☆ ☆ ☆ ☆ ☆

Wine Name _____

Winery _____ Region _____

When _____ Price _____ Alcohol % _____

Appearance _____ 🍷 🍷 🍷 🍷 🍷

Aroma _____ 🍷 🍷 🍷 🍷 🍷

Body _____ 🍷 🍷 🍷 🍷 🍷

Taste _____ 🍷 🍷 🍷 🍷 🍷

Finish _____ 🍷 🍷 🍷 🍷 🍷

Pairs With

Serving Temperature

Taste

Review / Notes

_____
_____
_____
_____
_____
_____
_____
_____
_____
_____

Ratings ☆ ☆ ☆ ☆ ☆

Wine Name _____

Winery _____ Region _____

When _____ Price _____ Alcohol % _____

Appearance _____ 🍷 🍷 🍷 🍷 🍷

Aroma _____ 🍷 🍷 🍷 🍷 🍷

Body _____ 🍷 🍷 🍷 🍷 🍷

Taste _____ 🍷 🍷 🍷 🍷 🍷

Finish _____ 🍷 🍷 🍷 🍷 🍷

Pairs With

Serving Temperature

Taste

Review / Notes

_____
_____
_____
_____
_____
_____
_____
_____
_____
_____

Ratings ☆ ☆ ☆ ☆ ☆

Wine Name _____

Winery _____ Region _____

When _____ Price _____ Alcohol % _____

Appearance _____ ♟ ♟ ♟ ♟ ♟

Aroma _____ ♟ ♟ ♟ ♟ ♟

Body _____ ♟ ♟ ♟ ♟ ♟

Taste _____ ♟ ♟ ♟ ♟ ♟

Finish _____ ♟ ♟ ♟ ♟ ♟

Pairs With

Serving Temperature

Taste

Review / Notes

_____
_____
_____
_____
_____
_____
_____
_____
_____
_____

Ratings ☆ ☆ ☆ ☆ ☆

Wine Name _____

Winery _____ Region _____

When _____ Price _____ Alcohol % _____

Appearance _____ ♙ ♙ ♙ ♙ ♙

Aroma _____ ♙ ♙ ♙ ♙ ♙

Body _____ ♙ ♙ ♙ ♙ ♙

Taste _____ ♙ ♙ ♙ ♙ ♙

Finish _____ ♙ ♙ ♙ ♙ ♙

--------- Pairs With --------- ┌── Serving Temperature ──┐ ── Taste ──

------------------------------ Review / Notes ------------------------------

_____

_____

_____

_____

_____

_____

_____

_____

_____

Ratings ☆ ☆ ☆ ☆ ☆

Wine Name _____

Winery _____ Region _____

When _____ Price _____ Alcohol % _____

Appearance _____ �glass �glass �glass ♛ ♛

Aroma _____ ♛ ♛ ♛ ♛ ♛

Body _____ ♛ ♛ ♛ ♛ ♛

Taste _____ ♛ ♛ ♛ ♛ ♛

Finish _____ ♛ ♛ ♛ ♛ ♛

Pairs With

Serving Temperature

Taste

Review / Notes

_____
_____
_____
_____
_____
_____
_____
_____
_____
_____

Ratings ☆ ☆ ☆ ☆ ☆

Wine Name _____

Winery _____ Region _____

When _____ Price _____ Alcohol % _____

Appearance _____ ♀ ♀ ♀ ♀ ♀

Aroma _____ ♀ ♀ ♀ ♀ ♀

Body _____ ♀ ♀ ♀ ♀ ♀

Taste _____ ♀ ♀ ♀ ♀ ♀

Finish _____ ♀ ♀ ♀ ♀ ♀

——— Pairs With ———   Serving Temperature   ——— Taste ———

——————————— Review / Notes ———————————

_____
_____
_____
_____
_____
_____
_____
_____
_____

Ratings ☆ ☆ ☆ ☆ ☆

Wine Name _____

Winery _____ Region _____

When _____ Price _____ Alcohol % _____

Appearance _____ ♀ ♀ ♀ ♀ ♀

Aroma _____ ♀ ♀ ♀ ♀ ♀

Body _____ ♀ ♀ ♀ ♀ ♀

Taste _____ ♀ ♀ ♀ ♀ ♀

Finish _____ ♀ ♀ ♀ ♀ ♀

Pairs With

Serving Temperature

Taste

Review / Notes

_____
_____
_____
_____
_____
_____
_____
_____
_____
_____

Ratings ☆ ☆ ☆ ☆ ☆

Wine Name _____

Winery _____ Region _____

When _____ Price _____ Alcohol % _____

Appearance _____ 🍷 🍷 🍷 🍷 🍷

Aroma _____ 🍷 🍷 🍷 🍷 🍷

Body _____ 🍷 🍷 🍷 🍷 🍷

Taste _____ 🍷 🍷 🍷 🍷 🍷

Finish _____ 🍷 🍷 🍷 🍷 🍷

Pairs With

Serving Temperature

Taste

Review / Notes

_____
_____
_____
_____
_____
_____
_____
_____
_____
_____

Ratings ☆ ☆ ☆ ☆ ☆

Wine Name _____

Winery _____ Region _____

When _____ Price _____ Alcohol % _____

Appearance _____ ♀ ♀ ♀ ♀ ♀

Aroma _____ ♀ ♀ ♀ ♀ ♀

Body _____ ♀ ♀ ♀ ♀ ♀

Taste _____ ♀ ♀ ♀ ♀ ♀

Finish _____ ♀ ♀ ♀ ♀ ♀

Pairs With

Serving Temperature

Taste

Review / Notes

_____
_____
_____
_____
_____
_____
_____
_____
_____
_____

Ratings ☆ ☆ ☆ ☆ ☆

Wine Name _____

Winery _____ Region _____

When _____ Price _____ Alcohol % _____

Appearance _____ ♟ ♟ ♟ ♟ ♟
Aroma _____ ♟ ♟ ♟ ♟ ♟
Body _____ ♟ ♟ ♟ ♟ ♟
Taste _____ ♟ ♟ ♟ ♟ ♟
Finish _____ ♟ ♟ ♟ ♟ ♟

Pairs With	Serving Temperature	Taste

Review / Notes

_____
_____
_____
_____
_____
_____
_____
_____
_____
_____

Ratings ☆ ☆ ☆ ☆ ☆

Wine Name _____

Winery _____ Region _____

When _____ Price _____ Alcohol % _____

Appearance _____ ♟ ♟ ♟ ♟ ♟
Aroma _____ ♟ ♟ ♟ ♟ ♟
Body _____ ♟ ♟ ♟ ♟ ♟
Taste _____ ♟ ♟ ♟ ♟ ♟
Finish _____ ♟ ♟ ♟ ♟ ♟

Pairs With

Serving Temperature

Taste

Review / Notes

_____
_____
_____
_____
_____
_____
_____
_____
_____
_____

Ratings ☆ ☆ ☆ ☆ ☆

Wine Name _____

Winery _____ Region _____

When _____ Price _____ Alcohol % _____

Appearance _____ ♟ ♟ ♟ ♟ ♟

Aroma _____ ♟ ♟ ♟ ♟ ♟

Body _____ ♟ ♟ ♟ ♟ ♟

Taste _____ ♟ ♟ ♟ ♟ ♟

Finish _____ ♟ ♟ ♟ ♟ ♟

—— Pairs With ——

—— Serving Temperature ——

—— Taste ——

—— Review / Notes ——

_____
_____
_____
_____
_____
_____
_____
_____
_____

Ratings ☆ ☆ ☆ ☆ ☆

Wine Name _____

Winery _____ Region _____

When _____ Price _____ Alcohol % _____

Appearance _____ �glass �glass �glass ♛ ♛

Aroma _____ ♛ ♛ ♛ ♛ ♛

Body _____ ♛ ♛ ♛ ♛ ♛

Taste _____ ♛ ♛ ♛ ♛ ♛

Finish _____ ♛ ♛ ♛ ♛ ♛

Pairs With

Serving Temperature

Taste

Review / Notes

_____
_____
_____
_____
_____
_____
_____
_____
_____
_____

Ratings ☆ ☆ ☆ ☆ ☆

Wine Name _____

Winery _____ Region _____

When _____ Price _____ Alcohol % _____

Appearance _____ 🍷 🍷 🍷 🍷 🍷

Aroma _____ 🍷 🍷 🍷 🍷 🍷

Body _____ 🍷 🍷 🍷 🍷 🍷

Taste _____ 🍷 🍷 🍷 🍷 🍷

Finish _____ 🍷 🍷 🍷 🍷 🍷

Pairs With

Serving Temperature

Taste

Review / Notes

_____

_____

_____

_____

_____

_____

_____

_____

_____

_____

Ratings ☆ ☆ ☆ ☆ ☆

Wine Name _____

Winery _____ Region _____

When _____ Price _____ Alcohol % _____

Appearance _____ 🍷 🍷 🍷 🍷 🍷

Aroma _____ 🍷 🍷 🍷 🍷 🍷

Body _____ 🍷 🍷 🍷 🍷 🍷

Taste _____ 🍷 🍷 🍷 🍷 🍷

Finish _____ 🍷 🍷 🍷 🍷 🍷

Pairs With

Serving Temperature

Taste

Review / Notes

_____
_____
_____
_____
_____
_____
_____
_____
_____
_____

Ratings ☆ ☆ ☆ ☆ ☆

Wine Name _____

Winery _____ Region _____

When _____ Price _____ Alcohol % _____

Appearance _____ ♟ ♟ ♟ ♟ ♟

Aroma _____ ♟ ♟ ♟ ♟ ♟

Body _____ ♟ ♟ ♟ ♟ ♟

Taste _____ ♟ ♟ ♟ ♟ ♟

Finish _____ ♟ ♟ ♟ ♟ ♟

—— Pairs With ——

Serving Temperature

—— Taste ——

———— Review / Notes ————

_____
_____
_____
_____
_____
_____
_____
_____
_____
_____

Ratings ☆ ☆ ☆ ☆ ☆

Wine Name _____

Winery _____ Region _____

When _____ Price _____ Alcohol % _____

Appearance _____ ♟ ♟ ♟ ♟ ♟

Aroma _____ ♟ ♟ ♟ ♟ ♟

Body _____ ♟ ♟ ♟ ♟ ♟

Taste _____ ♟ ♟ ♟ ♟ ♟

Finish _____ ♟ ♟ ♟ ♟ ♟

Pairs With

Serving Temperature

Taste

Review / Notes

_____
_____
_____
_____
_____
_____
_____
_____
_____
_____

Ratings ☆ ☆ ☆ ☆ ☆

Wine Name _____

Winery _____ Region _____

When _____ Price _____ Alcohol % _____

Appearance _____ ♟ ♟ ♟ ♟ ♟

Aroma _____ ♟ ♟ ♟ ♟ ♟

Body _____ ♟ ♟ ♟ ♟ ♟

Taste _____ ♟ ♟ ♟ ♟ ♟

Finish _____ ♟ ♟ ♟ ♟ ♟

——— Pairs With ———   ┌ Serving Temperature ┐   ——— Taste ———

——————————————— Review / Notes ———————————————

_____

_____

_____

_____

_____

_____

_____

_____

_____

Ratings ☆ ☆ ☆ ☆ ☆

Wine Name _____

Winery _____ Region _____

When _____ Price _____ Alcohol % _____

Appearance _____ ♟ ♟ ♟ ♟ ♟

Aroma _____ ♟ ♟ ♟ ♟ ♟

Body _____ ♟ ♟ ♟ ♟ ♟

Taste _____ ♟ ♟ ♟ ♟ ♟

Finish _____ ♟ ♟ ♟ ♟ ♟

Pairs With

Serving Temperature

Taste

Review / Notes

_____
_____
_____
_____
_____
_____
_____
_____
_____
_____

Ratings ☆ ☆ ☆ ☆ ☆

Wine Name _____

Winery _____ Region _____

When _____ Price _____ Alcohol % _____

Appearance _____ ♟ ♟ ♟ ♟ ♟

Aroma _____ ♟ ♟ ♟ ♟ ♟

Body _____ ♟ ♟ ♟ ♟ ♟

Taste _____ ♟ ♟ ♟ ♟ ♟

Finish _____ ♟ ♟ ♟ ♟ ♟

Pairs With

Serving Temperature

Taste

Review / Notes

_____
_____
_____
_____
_____
_____
_____
_____
_____
_____

Ratings ☆ ☆ ☆ ☆ ☆

Wine Name _____

Winery _____ Region _____

When _____ Price _____ Alcohol % _____

Appearance _____ ♀ ♀ ♀ ♀ ♀

Aroma _____ ♀ ♀ ♀ ♀ ♀

Body _____ ♀ ♀ ♀ ♀ ♀

Taste _____ ♀ ♀ ♀ ♀ ♀

Finish _____ ♀ ♀ ♀ ♀ ♀

Pairs With

Serving Temperature

Taste

Review / Notes

_____
_____
_____
_____
_____
_____
_____
_____
_____
_____

Ratings ☆ ☆ ☆ ☆ ☆

Wine Name _____

Winery _____ Region _____

When _____ Price _____ Alcohol % _____

Appearance _____ ♟ ♟ ♟ ♟ ♟

Aroma _____ ♟ ♟ ♟ ♟ ♟

Body _____ ♟ ♟ ♟ ♟ ♟

Taste _____ ♟ ♟ ♟ ♟ ♟

Finish _____ ♟ ♟ ♟ ♟ ♟

—— Pairs With ——	Serving Temperature	—— Taste ——

—————— Review / Notes ——————

_____
_____
_____
_____
_____
_____
_____
_____
_____

Ratings ☆ ☆ ☆ ☆ ☆

Wine Name _____

Winery _____ Region _____

When _____ Price _____ Alcohol % _____

Appearance _____ ♓ ♓ ♓ ♓ ♓

Aroma _____ ♓ ♓ ♓ ♓ ♓

Body _____ ♓ ♓ ♓ ♓ ♓

Taste _____ ♓ ♓ ♓ ♓ ♓

Finish _____ ♓ ♓ ♓ ♓ ♓

Pairs With

Serving Temperature

Taste

Review / Notes

_____

_____

_____

_____

_____

_____

_____

_____

_____

_____

Ratings ☆ ☆ ☆ ☆ ☆

Wine Name _____

Winery _____ Region _____

When _____ Price _____ Alcohol % _____

Appearance _____ ♟ ♟ ♟ ♟ ♟

Aroma _____ ♟ ♟ ♟ ♟ ♟

Body _____ ♟ ♟ ♟ ♟ ♟

Taste _____ ♟ ♟ ♟ ♟ ♟

Finish _____ ♟ ♟ ♟ ♟ ♟

—— Pairs With —— 　 Serving Temperature 　 —— Taste ——

—— Review / Notes ——

_____
_____
_____
_____
_____
_____
_____
_____
_____

Ratings ☆ ☆ ☆ ☆ ☆

Wine Name _____

Winery _____ Region _____

When _____ Price _____ Alcohol % _____

Appearance _____ ♀ ♀ ♀ ♀ ♀

Aroma _____ ♀ ♀ ♀ ♀ ♀

Body _____ ♀ ♀ ♀ ♀ ♀

Taste _____ ♀ ♀ ♀ ♀ ♀

Finish _____ ♀ ♀ ♀ ♀ ♀

—— Pairs With —— ⎡ Serving Temperature ⎤ —— Taste ——

—— Review / Notes ——

_____

_____

_____

_____

_____

_____

_____

_____

_____

_____

Ratings ☆ ☆ ☆ ☆ ☆

Wine Name _____

Winery _____ Region _____

When _____ Price _____ Alcohol % _____

Appearance _____ � � � � �

Aroma _____ � � � � �

Body _____ � � � � �

Taste _____ � � � � �

Finish _____ � � � � �

--- Pairs With ---

--- Serving Temperature ---

--- Taste ---

--- Review / Notes ---

_____
_____
_____
_____
_____
_____
_____
_____
_____
_____
_____

Ratings ☆ ☆ ☆ ☆ ☆

Wine Name _____

Winery _____ Region _____

When _____ Price _____ Alcohol % _____

Appearance _____ ♟ ♟ ♟ ♟ ♟

Aroma _____ ♟ ♟ ♟ ♟ ♟

Body _____ ♟ ♟ ♟ ♟ ♟

Taste _____ ♟ ♟ ♟ ♟ ♟

Finish _____ ♟ ♟ ♟ ♟ ♟

Pairs With

Serving Temperature

Taste

Review / Notes

_____
_____
_____
_____
_____
_____
_____
_____
_____
_____

Ratings ☆ ☆ ☆ ☆ ☆

Wine Name _____

Winery _____ Region _____

When _____ Price _____ Alcohol % _____

Appearance _____ 🍷 🍷 🍷 🍷 🍷

Aroma _____ 🍷 🍷 🍷 🍷 🍷

Body _____ 🍷 🍷 🍷 🍷 🍷

Taste _____ 🍷 🍷 🍷 🍷 🍷

Finish _____ 🍷 🍷 🍷 🍷 🍷

——— Pairs With ———   Serving Temperature   ——— Taste ———

——————————————— Review / Notes ———————————————

_____

_____

_____

_____

_____

_____

_____

_____

_____

Ratings ☆ ☆ ☆ ☆ ☆

Wine Name _____

Winery _____ Region _____

When _____ Price _____ Alcohol % _____

Appearance _____ 🍷 🍷 🍷 🍷 🍷

Aroma _____ 🍷 🍷 🍷 🍷 🍷

Body _____ 🍷 🍷 🍷 🍷 🍷

Taste _____ 🍷 🍷 🍷 🍷 🍷

Finish _____ 🍷 🍷 🍷 🍷 🍷

Pairs With

Serving Temperature

Taste

Review / Notes

_____
_____
_____
_____
_____
_____
_____
_____
_____
_____
_____

Ratings ☆ ☆ ☆ ☆ ☆

Wine Name _____

Winery _____ Region _____

When _____ Price _____ Alcohol % _____

Appearance _____ ♥ ♥ ♥ ♥ ♥

Aroma _____ ♥ ♥ ♥ ♥ ♥

Body _____ ♥ ♥ ♥ ♥ ♥

Taste _____ ♥ ♥ ♥ ♥ ♥

Finish _____ ♥ ♥ ♥ ♥ ♥

Pairs With	Serving Temperature	Taste

Review / Notes

_____
_____
_____
_____
_____
_____
_____
_____
_____
_____

Ratings ☆ ☆ ☆ ☆ ☆

Wine Name _____

Winery _____ Region _____

When _____ Price _____ Alcohol % _____

Appearance _____ ♀ ♀ ♀ ♀ ♀

Aroma _____ ♀ ♀ ♀ ♀ ♀

Body _____ ♀ ♀ ♀ ♀ ♀

Taste _____ ♀ ♀ ♀ ♀ ♀

Finish _____ ♀ ♀ ♀ ♀ ♀

--- Pairs With ---

--- Serving Temperature ---

--- Taste ---

--- Review / Notes ---

_____

_____

_____

_____

_____

_____

_____

_____

_____

_____

Ratings ☆ ☆ ☆ ☆ ☆

Wine Name _____

Winery _____ Region _____

When _____ Price _____ Alcohol % _____

Appearance _____ ♟ ♟ ♟ ♟ ♟

Aroma _____ ♟ ♟ ♟ ♟ ♟

Body _____ ♟ ♟ ♟ ♟ ♟

Taste _____ ♟ ♟ ♟ ♟ ♟

Finish _____ ♟ ♟ ♟ ♟ ♟

Pairs With

Serving Temperature

Taste

Review / Notes

_____

_____

_____

_____

_____

_____

_____

_____

_____

_____

Ratings ☆ ☆ ☆ ☆ ☆

Wine Name _____

Winery _____ Region _____

When _____ Price _____ Alcohol % _____

Appearance _____ ♥♥♥♥♥

Aroma _____ ♥♥♥♥♥

Body _____ ♥♥♥♥♥

Taste _____ ♥♥♥♥♥

Finish _____ ♥♥♥♥♥

Pairs With

Serving Temperature

Taste

Review / Notes

_____
_____
_____
_____
_____
_____
_____
_____
_____
_____

Ratings ☆ ☆ ☆ ☆ ☆

Wine Name _____

Winery _____ Region _____

When _____ Price _____ Alcohol % _____

Appearance _____ 🍷 🍷 🍷 🍷 🍷
Aroma _____ 🍷 🍷 🍷 🍷 🍷
Body _____ 🍷 🍷 🍷 🍷 🍷
Taste _____ 🍷 🍷 🍷 🍷 🍷
Finish _____ 🍷 🍷 🍷 🍷 🍷

─── Pairs With ───	Serving Temperature	─── Taste ───

─────── Review / Notes ───────

_____
_____
_____
_____
_____
_____
_____
_____
_____

Ratings ☆ ☆ ☆ ☆ ☆

Wine Name _____

Winery _____ Region _____

When _____ Price _____ Alcohol % _____

Appearance _____ ♟ ♟ ♟ ♟ ♟

Aroma _____ ♟ ♟ ♟ ♟ ♟

Body _____ ♟ ♟ ♟ ♟ ♟

Taste _____ ♟ ♟ ♟ ♟ ♟

Finish _____ ♟ ♟ ♟ ♟ ♟

Pairs With

Serving Temperature

Taste

Review / Notes

_____
_____
_____
_____
_____
_____
_____
_____
_____
_____
_____

Ratings ☆ ☆ ☆ ☆ ☆

Wine Name _____

Winery _____ Region _____

When _____ Price _____ Alcohol % _____

Appearance _____ ♀ ♀ ♀ ♀ ♀

Aroma _____ ♀ ♀ ♀ ♀ ♀

Body _____ ♀ ♀ ♀ ♀ ♀

Taste _____ ♀ ♀ ♀ ♀ ♀

Finish _____ ♀ ♀ ♀ ♀ ♀

Pairs With

Serving Temperature

Taste

Review / Notes

_____

_____

_____

_____

_____

_____

_____

_____

_____

Ratings ☆ ☆ ☆ ☆ ☆

Wine Name _____

Winery _____ Region _____

When _____ Price _____ Alcohol % _____

Appearance _____ ♀ ♀ ♀ ♀ ♀

Aroma _____ ♀ ♀ ♀ ♀ ♀

Body _____ ♀ ♀ ♀ ♀ ♀

Taste _____ ♀ ♀ ♀ ♀ ♀

Finish _____ ♀ ♀ ♀ ♀ ♀

--- Pairs With ---

--- Serving Temperature ---

--- Taste ---

--- Review / Notes ---

_____
_____
_____
_____
_____
_____
_____
_____
_____
_____

Ratings ☆ ☆ ☆ ☆ ☆

Wine Name _____

Winery _____ Region _____

When _____ Price _____ Alcohol % _____

Appearance _____ ♟ ♟ ♟ ♟ ♟

Aroma _____ ♟ ♟ ♟ ♟ ♟

Body _____ ♟ ♟ ♟ ♟ ♟

Taste _____ ♟ ♟ ♟ ♟ ♟

Finish _____ ♟ ♟ ♟ ♟ ♟

Pairs With

Serving Temperature

Taste

Review / Notes

_____
_____
_____
_____
_____
_____
_____
_____
_____
_____

Ratings ☆ ☆ ☆ ☆ ☆

Wine Name _____

Winery _____ Region _____

When _____ Price _____ Alcohol % _____

Appearance _____ ♟ ♟ ♟ ♟ ♟

Aroma _____ ♟ ♟ ♟ ♟ ♟

Body _____ ♟ ♟ ♟ ♟ ♟

Taste _____ ♟ ♟ ♟ ♟ ♟

Finish _____ ♟ ♟ ♟ ♟ ♟

Pairs With

Serving Temperature

Taste

Review / Notes

_____
_____
_____
_____
_____
_____
_____
_____
_____
_____

Ratings ☆ ☆ ☆ ☆ ☆

Wine Name _____

Winery _____ Region _____

When _____ Price _____ Alcohol % _____

Appearance _____ ♟ ♟ ♟ ♟ ♟

Aroma _____ ♟ ♟ ♟ ♟ ♟

Body _____ ♟ ♟ ♟ ♟ ♟

Taste _____ ♟ ♟ ♟ ♟ ♟

Finish _____ ♟ ♟ ♟ ♟ ♟

Pairs With

Serving Temperature

Taste

Review / Notes

_____
_____
_____
_____
_____
_____
_____
_____
_____
_____

Ratings ☆ ☆ ☆ ☆ ☆

Wine Name _____

Winery _____ Region _____

When _____ Price _____ Alcohol % _____

Appearance _____ ♟ ♟ ♟ ♟ ♟

Aroma _____ ♟ ♟ ♟ ♟ ♟

Body _____ ♟ ♟ ♟ ♟ ♟

Taste _____ ♟ ♟ ♟ ♟ ♟

Finish _____ ♟ ♟ ♟ ♟ ♟

┌──── Pairs With ────┐ ┌── Serving Temperature ──┐ ┌──── Taste ────

──── Review / Notes ────

_____

_____

_____

_____

_____

_____

_____

_____

_____

Ratings ☆ ☆ ☆ ☆ ☆

Wine Name _____

Winery _____ Region _____

When _____ Price _____ Alcohol % _____

Appearance _____ ♟ ♟ ♟ ♟ ♟

Aroma _____ ♟ ♟ ♟ ♟ ♟

Body _____ ♟ ♟ ♟ ♟ ♟

Taste _____ ♟ ♟ ♟ ♟ ♟

Finish _____ ♟ ♟ ♟ ♟ ♟

——— Pairs With ———

Serving Temperature

——— Taste ———

——————————————— Review / Notes ———————————————

_____
_____
_____
_____
_____
_____
_____
_____
_____

Ratings ☆ ☆ ☆ ☆ ☆

Wine Name _____

Winery _____ Region _____

When _____ Price _____ Alcohol % _____

Appearance _____ ♀ ♀ ♀ ♀ ♀

Aroma _____ ♀ ♀ ♀ ♀ ♀

Body _____ ♀ ♀ ♀ ♀ ♀

Taste _____ ♀ ♀ ♀ ♀ ♀

Finish _____ ♀ ♀ ♀ ♀ ♀

--- Pairs With ---

--- Serving Temperature ---

--- Taste ---

--- Review / Notes ---

_____
_____
_____
_____
_____
_____
_____
_____
_____
_____

Ratings ☆ ☆ ☆ ☆ ☆

Wine Name _____

Winery _____ Region _____

When _____ Price _____ Alcohol % _____

Appearance _____ ♟ ♟ ♟ ♟ ♟
Aroma _____ ♟ ♟ ♟ ♟ ♟
Body _____ ♟ ♟ ♟ ♟ ♟
Taste _____ ♟ ♟ ♟ ♟ ♟
Finish _____ ♟ ♟ ♟ ♟ ♟

Pairs With

Serving Temperature

Taste

Review / Notes

_____
_____
_____
_____
_____
_____
_____
_____
_____
_____

Ratings ☆ ☆ ☆ ☆ ☆

Wine Name _____

Winery _____ Region _____

When _____ Price _____ Alcohol % _____

Appearance _____ ♟ ♟ ♟ ♟ ♟

Aroma _____ ♟ ♟ ♟ ♟ ♟

Body _____ ♟ ♟ ♟ ♟ ♟

Taste _____ ♟ ♟ ♟ ♟ ♟

Finish _____ ♟ ♟ ♟ ♟ ♟

Pairs With

Serving Temperature

Taste

Review / Notes

_____
_____
_____
_____
_____
_____
_____
_____
_____
_____

Ratings ☆ ☆ ☆ ☆ ☆

Wine Name _____

Winery _____ Region _____

When _____ Price _____ Alcohol % _____

Appearance _____ 🍷 🍷 🍷 🍷 🍷

Aroma _____ 🍷 🍷 🍷 🍷 🍷

Body _____ 🍷 🍷 🍷 🍷 🍷

Taste _____ 🍷 🍷 🍷 🍷 🍷

Finish _____ 🍷 🍷 🍷 🍷 🍷

Pairs With

Serving Temperature

Taste

Review / Notes

_____
_____
_____
_____
_____
_____
_____
_____
_____
_____

Ratings ☆ ☆ ☆ ☆ ☆

Wine Name _____

Winery _____ Region _____

When _____ Price _____ Alcohol % _____

Appearance _____ ♟ ♟ ♟ ♟ ♟
Aroma _____ ♟ ♟ ♟ ♟ ♟
Body _____ ♟ ♟ ♟ ♟ ♟
Taste _____ ♟ ♟ ♟ ♟ ♟
Finish _____ ♟ ♟ ♟ ♟ ♟

—— Pairs With ——   —— Serving Temperature ——   —— Taste ——

—————————————— Review / Notes ——————————————

_____
_____
_____
_____
_____
_____
_____
_____
_____
_____

Ratings ☆ ☆ ☆ ☆ ☆

Wine Name _____

Winery _____ Region _____

When _____ Price _____ Alcohol % _____

Appearance _____ ♟ ♟ ♟ ♟ ♟

Aroma _____ ♟ ♟ ♟ ♟ ♟

Body _____ ♟ ♟ ♟ ♟ ♟

Taste _____ ♟ ♟ ♟ ♟ ♟

Finish _____ ♟ ♟ ♟ ♟ ♟

—— Pairs With —— | Serving Temperature | —— Taste ——

—————————— Review / Notes ——————————

_____

_____

_____

_____

_____

_____

_____

_____

_____

Ratings ☆ ☆ ☆ ☆ ☆

Wine Name _____

Winery _____ Region _____

When _____ Price _____ Alcohol % _____

Appearance _____ ♟ ♟ ♟ ♟ ♟

Aroma _____ ♟ ♟ ♟ ♟ ♟

Body _____ ♟ ♟ ♟ ♟ ♟

Taste _____ ♟ ♟ ♟ ♟ ♟

Finish _____ ♟ ♟ ♟ ♟ ♟

--- Pairs With ---

--- Serving Temperature ---

--- Taste ---

--- Review / Notes ---

_____

_____

_____

_____

_____

_____

_____

_____

_____

_____

Ratings ☆ ☆ ☆ ☆ ☆

Wine Name _____

Winery _____ Region _____

When _____ Price _____ Alcohol % _____

Appearance _____ ♁ ♁ ♁ ♁ ♁

Aroma _____ ♁ ♁ ♁ ♁ ♁

Body _____ ♁ ♁ ♁ ♁ ♁

Taste _____ ♁ ♁ ♁ ♁ ♁

Finish _____ ♁ ♁ ♁ ♁ ♁

--- Pairs With ---

--- Serving Temperature ---

--- Taste ---

--- Review / Notes ---

_____
_____
_____
_____
_____
_____
_____
_____
_____
_____

Ratings ☆ ☆ ☆ ☆ ☆

Wine Name _____

Winery _____ Region _____

When _____ Price _____ Alcohol % _____

Appearance _____ 🍷 🍷 🍷 🍷 🍷

Aroma _____ 🍷 🍷 🍷 🍷 🍷

Body _____ 🍷 🍷 🍷 🍷 🍷

Taste _____ 🍷 🍷 🍷 🍷 🍷

Finish _____ 🍷 🍷 🍷 🍷 🍷

Pairs With

Serving Temperature

Taste

Review / Notes

_____
_____
_____
_____
_____
_____
_____
_____
_____
_____

Ratings ☆ ☆ ☆ ☆ ☆

Wine Name _____

Winery _____ Region _____

When _____ Price _____ Alcohol % _____

Appearance _____ 🍷 🍷 🍷 🍷 🍷

Aroma _____ 🍷 🍷 🍷 🍷 🍷

Body _____ 🍷 🍷 🍷 🍷 🍷

Taste _____ 🍷 🍷 🍷 🍷 🍷

Finish _____ 🍷 🍷 🍷 🍷 🍷

—— Pairs With ——

—— Serving Temperature ——

—— Taste ——

—— Review / Notes ——

_____
_____
_____
_____
_____
_____
_____
_____
_____

Ratings ☆ ☆ ☆ ☆ ☆

Wine Name _____

Winery _____ Region _____

When _____ Price _____ Alcohol % _____

Appearance _____ ♟ ♟ ♟ ♟ ♟

Aroma _____ ♟ ♟ ♟ ♟ ♟

Body _____ ♟ ♟ ♟ ♟ ♟

Taste _____ ♟ ♟ ♟ ♟ ♟

Finish _____ ♟ ♟ ♟ ♟ ♟

Pairs With

Serving Temperature

Taste

Review / Notes

_____
_____
_____
_____
_____
_____
_____
_____
_____
_____

Ratings ☆ ☆ ☆ ☆ ☆

Wine Name _____

Winery _____ Region _____

When _____ Price _____ Alcohol % _____

Appearance _____ ♟ ♟ ♟ ♟ ♟

Aroma _____ ♟ ♟ ♟ ♟ ♟

Body _____ ♟ ♟ ♟ ♟ ♟

Taste _____ ♟ ♟ ♟ ♟ ♟

Finish _____ ♟ ♟ ♟ ♟ ♟

——— Pairs With ——— ——— Serving Temperature ——— ——— Taste ———

——————————————— Review / Notes ———————————————

_____
_____
_____
_____
_____
_____
_____
_____
_____

Ratings ☆ ☆ ☆ ☆ ☆

Wine Name _____

Winery _____ Region _____

When _____ Price _____ Alcohol % _____

Appearance _____ ♀ ♀ ♀ ♀ ♀

Aroma _____ ♀ ♀ ♀ ♀ ♀

Body _____ ♀ ♀ ♀ ♀ ♀

Taste _____ ♀ ♀ ♀ ♀ ♀

Finish _____ ♀ ♀ ♀ ♀ ♀

── Pairs With ──   ── Serving Temperature ──   ── Taste ──

──────── Review / Notes ────────

_____
_____
_____
_____
_____
_____
_____
_____
_____
_____

Ratings ☆ ☆ ☆ ☆ ☆

Wine Name _____

Winery _____ Region _____

When _____ Price _____ Alcohol % _____

Appearance _____ ♟ ♟ ♟ ♟ ♟
Aroma _____ ♟ ♟ ♟ ♟ ♟
Body _____ ♟ ♟ ♟ ♟ ♟
Taste _____ ♟ ♟ ♟ ♟ ♟
Finish _____ ♟ ♟ ♟ ♟ ♟

Pairs With

Serving Temperature

Taste

Review / Notes

_____
_____
_____
_____
_____
_____
_____
_____
_____
_____

Ratings ☆ ☆ ☆ ☆ ☆

Wine Name _____

Winery _____ Region _____

When _____ Price _____ Alcohol % _____

Appearance _____ ♟ ♟ ♟ ♟ ♟

Aroma _____ ♟ ♟ ♟ ♟ ♟

Body _____ ♟ ♟ ♟ ♟ ♟

Taste _____ ♟ ♟ ♟ ♟ ♟

Finish _____ ♟ ♟ ♟ ♟ ♟

Pairs With	Serving Temperature	Taste

Review / Notes

_____

_____

_____

_____

_____

_____

_____

_____

_____

_____

Ratings ☆ ☆ ☆ ☆ ☆

Wine Name _____

Winery _____ Region _____

When _____ Price _____ Alcohol % _____

Appearance _____ ♀ ♀ ♀ ♀ ♀

Aroma _____ ♀ ♀ ♀ ♀ ♀

Body _____ ♀ ♀ ♀ ♀ ♀

Taste _____ ♀ ♀ ♀ ♀ ♀

Finish _____ ♀ ♀ ♀ ♀ ♀

Pairs With

Serving Temperature

Taste

Review / Notes

_____
_____
_____
_____
_____
_____
_____
_____
_____

Ratings ☆ ☆ ☆ ☆ ☆

Wine Name _____

Winery _____ Region _____

When _____ Price _____ Alcohol % _____

Appearance _____ ♟ ♟ ♟ ♟ ♟
Aroma _____ ♟ ♟ ♟ ♟ ♟
Body _____ ♟ ♟ ♟ ♟ ♟
Taste _____ ♟ ♟ ♟ ♟ ♟
Finish _____ ♟ ♟ ♟ ♟ ♟

Pairs With

Serving Temperature

Taste

Review / Notes

_____
_____
_____
_____
_____
_____
_____
_____
_____
_____

Ratings ☆ ☆ ☆ ☆ ☆

Wine Name _____

Winery _____ Region _____

When _____ Price _____ Alcohol % _____

Appearance _____ ♟ ♟ ♟ ♟ ♟

Aroma _____ ♟ ♟ ♟ ♟ ♟

Body _____ ♟ ♟ ♟ ♟ ♟

Taste _____ ♟ ♟ ♟ ♟ ♟

Finish _____ ♟ ♟ ♟ ♟ ♟

Pairs With	Serving Temperature	Taste

Review / Notes

_____

_____

_____

_____

_____

_____

_____

_____

Ratings ☆ ☆ ☆ ☆ ☆

Wine Name _____

Winery _____ Region _____

When _____ Price _____ Alcohol % _____

Appearance _____ ♟ ♟ ♟ ♟ ♟

Aroma _____ ♟ ♟ ♟ ♟ ♟

Body _____ ♟ ♟ ♟ ♟ ♟

Taste _____ ♟ ♟ ♟ ♟ ♟

Finish _____ ♟ ♟ ♟ ♟ ♟

Pairs With

Serving Temperature

Taste

Review / Notes

_____
_____
_____
_____
_____
_____
_____
_____
_____
_____

Ratings ☆ ☆ ☆ ☆ ☆

Wine Name _____

Winery _____ Region _____

When _____ Price _____ Alcohol % _____

Appearance _____ ♟ ♟ ♟ ♟ ♟

Aroma _____ ♟ ♟ ♟ ♟ ♟

Body _____ ♟ ♟ ♟ ♟ ♟

Taste _____ ♟ ♟ ♟ ♟ ♟

Finish _____ ♟ ♟ ♟ ♟ ♟

Pairs With

Serving Temperature

Taste

Review / Notes

_____

_____

_____

_____

_____

_____

_____

_____

_____

Ratings ☆ ☆ ☆ ☆ ☆

Wine Name _____

Winery _____ Region _____

When _____ Price _____ Alcohol % _____

Appearance _____ 🍷 🍷 🍷 🍷 🍷

Aroma _____ 🍷 🍷 🍷 🍷 🍷

Body _____ 🍷 🍷 🍷 🍷 🍷

Taste _____ 🍷 🍷 🍷 🍷 🍷

Finish _____ 🍷 🍷 🍷 🍷 🍷

Pairs With

Serving Temperature

Taste

Review / Notes

_____
_____
_____
_____
_____
_____
_____
_____
_____
_____

Ratings ☆ ☆ ☆ ☆ ☆

Wine Name _____

Winery _____ Region _____

When _____ Price _____ Alcohol % _____

Appearance _____ 🍷 🍷 🍷 🍷 🍷

Aroma _____ 🍷 🍷 🍷 🍷 🍷

Body _____ 🍷 🍷 🍷 🍷 🍷

Taste _____ 🍷 🍷 🍷 🍷 🍷

Finish _____ 🍷 🍷 🍷 🍷 🍷

——— Pairs With ———

——— Serving Temperature ———

——— Taste ———

——— Review / Notes ———

_____
_____
_____
_____
_____
_____
_____
_____
_____

Ratings ☆ ☆ ☆ ☆ ☆

Wine Name _____

Winery _____ Region _____

When _____ Price _____ Alcohol % _____

Appearance _____ ♟ ♟ ♟ ♟ ♟

Aroma _____ ♟ ♟ ♟ ♟ ♟

Body _____ ♟ ♟ ♟ ♟ ♟

Taste _____ ♟ ♟ ♟ ♟ ♟

Finish _____ ♟ ♟ ♟ ♟ ♟

Pairs With	Serving Temperature	Taste

Review / Notes

_____
_____
_____
_____
_____
_____
_____
_____
_____
_____

Ratings ☆ ☆ ☆ ☆ ☆

Wine Name _____

Winery _____ Region _____

When _____ Price _____ Alcohol % _____

Appearance _____ ♥ ♥ ♥ ♥ ♥

Aroma _____ ♥ ♥ ♥ ♥ ♥

Body _____ ♥ ♥ ♥ ♥ ♥

Taste _____ ♥ ♥ ♥ ♥ ♥

Finish _____ ♥ ♥ ♥ ♥ ♥

──── Pairs With ────   ── Serving Temperature ──   ──── Taste ────

──────── Review / Notes ────────

_____
_____
_____
_____
_____
_____
_____
_____
_____
_____

Ratings ☆ ☆ ☆ ☆ ☆

Wine Name _____

Winery _____ Region _____

When _____ Price _____ Alcohol % _____

Appearance _____ �glasses (5)
Aroma _____ �glasses (5)
Body _____ ♛ ♛ ♛ ♛ ♛
Taste _____ ♛ ♛ ♛ ♛ ♛
Finish _____ ♛ ♛ ♛ ♛ ♛

--- Pairs With --- | --- Serving Temperature --- | --- Taste ---

--- Review / Notes ---

_____
_____
_____
_____
_____
_____
_____
_____
_____
_____

Ratings ☆ ☆ ☆ ☆ ☆

Wine Name _____

Winery _____ Region _____

When _____ Price _____ Alcohol % _____

Appearance _____ ♟♟♟♟♟
Aroma _____ ♟♟♟♟♟
Body _____ ♟♟♟♟♟
Taste _____ ♟♟♟♟♟
Finish _____ ♟♟♟♟♟

Pairs With

Serving Temperature

Taste

Review / Notes

_____
_____
_____
_____
_____
_____
_____
_____
_____
_____

Ratings ☆ ☆ ☆ ☆ ☆

Wine Name _____

Winery _____ Region _____

When _____ Price _____ Alcohol % _____

Appearance _____ 🍷 🍷 🍷 🍷 🍷

Aroma _____ 🍷 🍷 🍷 🍷 🍷

Body _____ 🍷 🍷 🍷 🍷 🍷

Taste _____ 🍷 🍷 🍷 🍷 🍷

Finish _____ 🍷 🍷 🍷 🍷 🍷

Pairs With

Serving Temperature

Taste

Review / Notes

_____
_____
_____
_____
_____
_____
_____
_____
_____
_____

Ratings ☆ ☆ ☆ ☆ ☆

Wine Name _____

Winery _____ Region _____

When _____ Price _____ Alcohol % _____

Appearance _____ ♟ ♟ ♟ ♟ ♟
Aroma _____ ♟ ♟ ♟ ♟ ♟
Body _____ ♟ ♟ ♟ ♟ ♟
Taste _____ ♟ ♟ ♟ ♟ ♟
Finish _____ ♟ ♟ ♟ ♟ ♟

──── Pairs With ────   Serving Temperature   ──── Taste ────

──────────────── Review / Notes ────────────────

_____
_____
_____
_____
_____
_____
_____
_____
_____

Ratings ☆ ☆ ☆ ☆ ☆

Wine Name _____

Winery _____ Region _____

When _____ Price _____ Alcohol % _____

Appearance _____ ♟ ♟ ♟ ♟ ♟
Aroma _____ ♟ ♟ ♟ ♟ ♟
Body _____ ♟ ♟ ♟ ♟ ♟
Taste _____ ♟ ♟ ♟ ♟ ♟
Finish _____ ♟ ♟ ♟ ♟ ♟

——— Pairs With ———   ——— Serving Temperature ———   ——— Taste ———

——— Review / Notes ———

_____
_____
_____
_____
_____
_____
_____
_____
_____
_____

Ratings ☆ ☆ ☆ ☆ ☆

Wine Name _____

Winery _____ Region _____

When _____ Price _____ Alcohol % _____

Appearance _____ 🍷 🍷 🍷 🍷 🍷

Aroma _____ 🍷 🍷 🍷 🍷 🍷

Body _____ 🍷 🍷 🍷 🍷 🍷

Taste _____ 🍷 🍷 🍷 🍷 🍷

Finish _____ 🍷 🍷 🍷 🍷 🍷

Pairs With

Serving Temperature

Taste

Review / Notes

_____
_____
_____
_____
_____
_____
_____
_____
_____
_____

Ratings ☆ ☆ ☆ ☆ ☆

Wine Name _____

Winery _____ Region _____

When _____ Price _____ Alcohol % _____

Appearance _____ ♟ ♟ ♟ ♟ ♟

Aroma _____ ♟ ♟ ♟ ♟ ♟

Body _____ ♟ ♟ ♟ ♟ ♟

Taste _____ ♟ ♟ ♟ ♟ ♟

Finish _____ ♟ ♟ ♟ ♟ ♟

--- Pairs With ---

--- Serving Temperature ---

--- Taste ---

--- Review / Notes ---

_____
_____
_____
_____
_____
_____
_____
_____
_____
_____

Ratings ☆ ☆ ☆ ☆ ☆

Wine Name _____

Winery _____ Region _____

When _____ Price _____ Alcohol % _____

Appearance _____ 🍷 🍷 🍷 🍷 🍷

Aroma _____ 🍷 🍷 🍷 🍷 🍷

Body _____ 🍷 🍷 🍷 🍷 🍷

Taste _____ 🍷 🍷 🍷 🍷 🍷

Finish _____ 🍷 🍷 🍷 🍷 🍷

Pairs With

Serving Temperature

Taste

Review / Notes

_____
_____
_____
_____
_____
_____
_____
_____
_____
_____

Ratings ☆ ☆ ☆ ☆ ☆

Wine Name _____

Winery _____ Region _____

When _____ Price _____ Alcohol % _____

Appearance _____ 🍷 🍷 🍷 🍷 🍷

Aroma _____ 🍷 🍷 🍷 🍷 🍷

Body _____ 🍷 🍷 🍷 🍷 🍷

Taste _____ 🍷 🍷 🍷 🍷 🍷

Finish _____ 🍷 🍷 🍷 🍷 🍷

Pairs With

Serving Temperature

Taste

Review / Notes

_____
_____
_____
_____
_____
_____
_____
_____
_____
_____

Ratings ☆ ☆ ☆ ☆ ☆

Wine Name _____

Winery _____ Region _____

When _____ Price _____ Alcohol % _____

Appearance _____ 🍷 🍷 🍷 🍷 🍷

Aroma _____ 🍷 🍷 🍷 🍷 🍷

Body _____ 🍷 🍷 🍷 🍷 🍷

Taste _____ 🍷 🍷 🍷 🍷 🍷

Finish _____ 🍷 🍷 🍷 🍷 🍷

Pairs With

Serving Temperature

Taste

Review / Notes

_____
_____
_____
_____
_____
_____
_____
_____
_____

Ratings ☆ ☆ ☆ ☆ ☆

Wine Name _____

Winery _____ Region _____

When _____ Price _____ Alcohol % _____

Appearance _____ ♟ ♟ ♟ ♟ ♟

Aroma _____ ♟ ♟ ♟ ♟ ♟

Body _____ ♟ ♟ ♟ ♟ ♟

Taste _____ ♟ ♟ ♟ ♟ ♟

Finish _____ ♟ ♟ ♟ ♟ ♟

Pairs With

Serving Temperature

Taste

Review / Notes

_____
_____
_____
_____
_____
_____
_____
_____
_____
_____

Ratings ☆ ☆ ☆ ☆ ☆

Wine Name _____

Winery _____ Region _____

When _____ Price _____ Alcohol % _____

Appearance _____ ♛ ♛ ♛ ♛ ♛

Aroma _____ ♛ ♛ ♛ ♛ ♛

Body _____ ♛ ♛ ♛ ♛ ♛

Taste _____ ♛ ♛ ♛ ♛ ♛

Finish _____ ♛ ♛ ♛ ♛ ♛

Pairs With

Serving Temperature

Taste

Review / Notes

_____
_____
_____
_____
_____
_____
_____
_____
_____
_____

Ratings ☆ ☆ ☆ ☆ ☆

Wine Name _____

Winery _____ Region _____

When _____ Price _____ Alcohol % _____

Appearance _____ ♟ ♟ ♟ ♟ ♟

Aroma _____ ♟ ♟ ♟ ♟ ♟

Body _____ ♟ ♟ ♟ ♟ ♟

Taste _____ ♟ ♟ ♟ ♟ ♟

Finish _____ ♟ ♟ ♟ ♟ ♟

—— Pairs With ——   —— Serving Temperature ——   —— Taste ——

—————————————————— Review / Notes ——————————————————

_____

_____

_____

_____

_____

_____

_____

_____

_____

_____

Ratings ☆ ☆ ☆ ☆ ☆

Wine Name _____

Winery _____ Region _____

When _____ Price _____ Alcohol % _____

Appearance _____ 🍷 🍷 🍷 🍷 🍷

Aroma _____ 🍷 🍷 🍷 🍷 🍷

Body _____ 🍷 🍷 🍷 🍷 🍷

Taste _____ 🍷 🍷 🍷 🍷 🍷

Finish _____ 🍷 🍷 🍷 🍷 🍷

Pairs With

Serving Temperature

Taste

Review / Notes

_____

_____

_____

_____

_____

_____

_____

_____

_____

_____

Ratings ☆ ☆ ☆ ☆ ☆

Wine Name _____

Winery _____ Region _____

When _____ Price _____ Alcohol % _____

Appearance _____ 🍷 🍷 🍷 🍷 🍷

Aroma _____ 🍷 🍷 🍷 🍷 🍷

Body _____ 🍷 🍷 🍷 🍷 🍷

Taste _____ 🍷 🍷 🍷 🍷 🍷

Finish _____ 🍷 🍷 🍷 🍷 🍷

Pairs With

Serving Temperature

Taste

Review / Notes

Ratings ☆ ☆ ☆ ☆ ☆

Wine Name _____

Winery _____ Region _____

When _____ Price _____ Alcohol % _____

Appearance _____ ♟ ♟ ♟ ♟ ♟

Aroma _____ ♟ ♟ ♟ ♟ ♟

Body _____ ♟ ♟ ♟ ♟ ♟

Taste _____ ♟ ♟ ♟ ♟ ♟

Finish _____ ♟ ♟ ♟ ♟ ♟

—— Pairs With ——

—— Serving Temperature ——

—— Taste ——

—— Review / Notes ——

_____

_____

_____

_____

_____

_____

_____

_____

_____

_____

Ratings ☆ ☆ ☆ ☆ ☆

Wine Name _____

Winery _____ Region _____

When _____ Price _____ Alcohol % _____

Appearance _____ ♟ ♟ ♟ ♟ ♟

Aroma _____ ♟ ♟ ♟ ♟ ♟

Body _____ ♟ ♟ ♟ ♟ ♟

Taste _____ ♟ ♟ ♟ ♟ ♟

Finish _____ ♟ ♟ ♟ ♟ ♟

Pairs With

Serving Temperature

Taste

Review / Notes

_____
_____
_____
_____
_____
_____
_____
_____
_____
_____

Ratings ☆ ☆ ☆ ☆ ☆

Wine Name _____

Winery _____ Region _____

When _____ Price _____ Alcohol % _____

Appearance _____ 🍷 🍷 🍷 🍷 🍷

Aroma _____ 🍷 🍷 🍷 🍷 🍷

Body _____ 🍷 🍷 🍷 🍷 🍷

Taste _____ 🍷 🍷 🍷 🍷 🍷

Finish _____ 🍷 🍷 🍷 🍷 🍷

─── Pairs With ───	─ Serving Temperature ─	─── Taste ───

─────── Review / Notes ───────

_____
_____
_____
_____
_____
_____
_____
_____
_____

Ratings ☆ ☆ ☆ ☆ ☆

Wine Name _____

Winery _____ Region _____

When _____ Price _____ Alcohol % _____

Appearance _____ ♟ ♟ ♟ ♟ ♟

Aroma _____ ♟ ♟ ♟ ♟ ♟

Body _____ ♟ ♟ ♟ ♟ ♟

Taste _____ ♟ ♟ ♟ ♟ ♟

Finish _____ ♟ ♟ ♟ ♟ ♟

┌─── Pairs With ───┐ ┌─ Serving Temperature ─┐ ┌─ Taste ─┐

┌─────────────── Review / Notes ───────────────┐

_____

_____

_____

_____

_____

_____

_____

_____

_____

_____

Ratings ☆ ☆ ☆ ☆ ☆

Wine Name _____

Winery _____ Region _____

When _____ Price _____ Alcohol % _____

Appearance _____ ♟ ♟ ♟ ♟ ♟
Aroma _____ ♟ ♟ ♟ ♟ ♟
Body _____ ♟ ♟ ♟ ♟ ♟
Taste _____ ♟ ♟ ♟ ♟ ♟
Finish _____ ♟ ♟ ♟ ♟ ♟

Pairs With

Serving Temperature

Taste

Review / Notes

_____
_____
_____
_____
_____
_____
_____
_____
_____
_____

Ratings ☆ ☆ ☆ ☆ ☆

Wine Name _____

Winery _____ Region _____

When _____ Price _____ Alcohol % _____

Appearance _____ ♂ ♂ ♂ ♂ ♂

Aroma _____ ♂ ♂ ♂ ♂ ♂

Body _____ ♂ ♂ ♂ ♂ ♂

Taste _____ ♂ ♂ ♂ ♂ ♂

Finish _____ ♂ ♂ ♂ ♂ ♂

Pairs With

Serving Temperature

Taste

Review / Notes

_____
_____
_____
_____
_____
_____
_____
_____
_____
_____

Ratings ☆ ☆ ☆ ☆ ☆

Wine Name _____

Winery _____ Region _____

When _____ Price _____ Alcohol % _____

Appearance _____ ♟ ♟ ♟ ♟ ♟

Aroma _____ ♟ ♟ ♟ ♟ ♟

Body _____ ♟ ♟ ♟ ♟ ♟

Taste _____ ♟ ♟ ♟ ♟ ♟

Finish _____ ♟ ♟ ♟ ♟ ♟

─── Pairs With ───	─── Serving Temperature ───	─── Taste ───

─────────────── Review / Notes ───────────────

_____

_____

_____

_____

_____

_____

_____

_____

_____

Ratings ☆ ☆ ☆ ☆ ☆

Are you enjoying this awesome Wine Journal?

If so, please leave us a review. We are very interested in your feedback to create even better products for you to enjoy in the near future.

Shopping for Weekly & Monthly Planners can be fun. Visit our website at amazing-notebooks.com or scan the QR code below to see all of our awesome and creative products!

Thank you very much!

Amazing Notebooks & Journals

www.amazing-notebooks.com

Copyright © 2019. All rights reserved.

Printed in Great Britain
by Amazon